Masonry farther dissected; or, more secrets of that mysterious society reveal'd. Faithfully Englished from the French original just publish'd at Paris, ... With explanatory notes ... by the translator. Likewise, an appendix, ...

ECCO

PRINT EDITIONS

Masonry farther dissected; or, more secrets of that mysterious society reveal'd. Faithfully Englished from the French original just publish'd at Paris, ... With explanatory notes ... by the translator. Likewise, an appendix, ...

Multiple Contributors, See Notes
ESTCID: T095603
Reproduction from British Library
Intended as a sequel to S. Prichard's 'Masonry dissected'.
London : printed for J. Wilford, 1738.
32p. ; 8°

Gale ECCO Print Editions

Relive history with *Eighteenth Century Collections Online,* now available in print for the independent historian and collector. This series includes the most significant English-language and foreign-language works printed in Great Britain during the eighteenth century, and is organized in seven different subject areas including literature and language; medicine, science, and technology; and religion and philosophy. The collection also includes thousands of important works from the Americas.

The eighteenth century has been called "The Age of Enlightenment." It was a period of rapid advance in print culture and publishing, in world exploration, and in the rapid growth of science and technology – all of which had a profound impact on the political and cultural landscape. At the end of the century the American Revolution, French Revolution and Industrial Revolution, perhaps three of the most significant events in modern history, set in motion developments that eventually dominated world political, economic, and social life.

In a groundbreaking effort, Gale initiated a revolution of its own: digitization of epic proportions to preserve these invaluable works in the largest online archive of its kind. Contributions from major world libraries constitute over 175,000 original printed works. Scanned images of the actual pages, rather than transcriptions, recreate the works *as they first appeared.*

Now for the first time, these high-quality digital scans of original works are available via print-on-demand, making them readily accessible to libraries, students, independent scholars, and readers of all ages.

For our initial release we have created seven robust collections to form one the world's most comprehensive catalogs of 18th century works.

Initial Gale ECCO Print Editions collections include:

History and Geography
Rich in titles on English life and social history, this collection spans the world as it was known to eighteenth-century historians and explorers. Titles include a wealth of travel accounts and diaries, histories of nations from throughout the world, and maps and charts of a world that was still being discovered. Students of the War of American Independence will find fascinating accounts from the British side of conflict.

Social Science

Delve into what it was like to live during the eighteenth century by reading the first-hand accounts of everyday people, including city dwellers and farmers, businessmen and bankers, artisans and merchants, artists and their patrons, politicians and their constituents. Original texts make the American, French, and Industrial revolutions vividly contemporary.

Medicine, Science and Technology

Medical theory and practice of the 1700s developed rapidly, as is evidenced by the extensive collection, which includes descriptions of diseases, their conditions, and treatments. Books on science and technology, agriculture, military technology, natural philosophy, even cookbooks, are all contained here.

Literature and Language

Western literary study flows out of eighteenth-century works by Alexander Pope, Daniel Defoe, Henry Fielding, Frances Burney, Denis Diderot, Johann Gottfried Herder, Johann Wolfgang von Goethe, and others. Experience the birth of the modern novel, or compare the development of language using dictionaries and grammar discourses.

Religion and Philosophy

The Age of Enlightenment profoundly enriched religious and philosophical understanding and continues to influence present-day thinking. Works collected here include masterpieces by David Hume, Immanuel Kant, and Jean-Jacques Rousseau, as well as religious sermons and moral debates on the issues of the day, such as the slave trade. The Age of Reason saw conflict between Protestantism and Catholicism transformed into one between faith and logic -- a debate that continues in the twenty-first century.

Law and Reference

This collection reveals the history of English common law and Empire law in a vastly changing world of British expansion. Dominating the legal field is the *Commentaries of the Law of England* by Sir William Blackstone, which first appeared in 1765. Reference works such as almanacs and catalogues continue to educate us by revealing the day-to-day workings of society.

Fine Arts

The eighteenth-century fascination with Greek and Roman antiquity followed the systematic excavation of the ruins at Pompeii and Herculaneum in southern Italy; and after 1750 a neoclassical style dominated all artistic fields. The titles here trace developments in mostly English-language works on painting, sculpture, architecture, music, theater, and other disciplines. Instructional works on musical instruments, catalogs of art objects, comic operas, and more are also included.

The BiblioLife Network

This project was made possible in part by the BiblioLife Network (BLN), a project aimed at addressing some of the huge challenges facing book preservationists around the world. The BLN includes libraries, library networks, archives, subject matter experts, online communities and library service providers. We believe every book ever published should be available as a high-quality print reproduction; printed on-demand anywhere in the world. This insures the ongoing accessibility of the content and helps generate sustainable revenue for the libraries and organizations that work to preserve these important materials.

The following book is in the "public domain" and represents an authentic reproduction of the text as printed by the original publisher. While we have attempted to accurately maintain the integrity of the original work, there are sometimes problems with the original work or the micro-film from which the books were digitized. This can result in minor errors in reproduction. Possible imperfections include missing and blurred pages, poor pictures, markings and other reproduction issues beyond our control. Because this work is culturally important, we have made it available as part of our commitment to protecting, preserving, and promoting the world's literature.

GUIDE TO FOLD-OUTS MAPS and OVERSIZED IMAGES

The book you are reading was digitized from microfilm captured over the past thirty to forty years. Years after the creation of the original microfilm, the book was converted to digital files and made available in an online database.

In an online database, page images do not need to conform to the size restrictions found in a printed book. When converting these images back into a printed bound book, the page sizes are standardized in ways that maintain the detail of the original. For large images, such as fold-out maps, the original page image is split into two or more pages

Guidelines used to determine how to split the page image follows:

• Some images are split vertically; large images require vertical and horizontal splits.
• For horizontal splits, the content is split left to right.
• For vertical splits, the content is split from top to bottom.
• For both vertical and horizontal splits, the image is processed from top left to bottom right.

MASONRY *farther* DISSECTED;

OR, MORE

SECRETS

Of that Mysterious

SOCIETY

REVEAL'D.

Faithfully *Englished* from the *French* Original just publish'd at *Paris*, by the *Permission* and *Privilege* of M. DE HARRAUT, Lieutenant-General of *Police*.

With Explanatory NOTES (both serious and comical) by the TRANSLATOR.

Likewise,

An APPENDIX, wherein are contain'd,

I The *Free-Masons* Reception in Foreign Parts
II The *Free-Masons* Apology, as publish'd at *Paris*.
III. *Free-Masons* a dangerous Society, from the *CRAFTSMAN*

LONDON:

Printed for *J. Wilford*, at the *Three Golden Flower-de-Luces*, behind the *Chapter-House*, near St *Paul's*. 1738 (Pr 6d)
Where may be had,
Masonry Dissected The Seventh Edition Pr 6d.

MASONRY

FARTHER

DISSECTED.

 HE Party muft firft of all be propos'd to the *Lodge*, by a Member thereof, as a Perfon worthy Admittance into the Society.

Anfwer being made, That he be admitted to prefent himfelf;

A 2   The

The Recipiendary, or Candidate, is then conducted by the Propoſer (*a*) (who becomes, as we may ſay, his *Parain*, or God-Father, into a Room without Light, in the ſame Houſe where the Lodge is, and is there ask-ed, *Whether he has a* Call *to be re-ceiv'd?* (*b*)

If he anſwers *Yes*; they then inter-rogate him concerning his Name, his Sur-name, his Quality, &c.

Then they take away whatever he has of Metal about him, as Buckles, Buttons, Rings, Boxes, &c. (*c*)

This done, they bare his right Knee; make him put his left Shoe down at Heel,

---

(*a*) Accompanied by ſome Brethren Aſſiſtants, as evidently appears by the Sequel.

(*b* *i. e.* Whether he be deſirous to become a *Maſon.*

(*c*) This, I have been told, they phraſe, *De-priving him of Metal.* They take even his Mo-ney; but all is punctually reſtor'd.

Heel, and wear it flip-fhod; blind-fold his Eyes; (*d*) and in this Plight keep him to contemplate on the Mat-ter, for about a Quarter of an Hour.

The God-Father, on leaving his God-Son in that State of Obfcurity and Darknefs goes and knocks thrice at the Lodge-Room Door, where (*e*) the venerable Grand-Mafter, with

(*d*) With a clean Napkin, or Handkerchief, as we may prefume. They hold, like other Sccta-ries, all who are not *Fre -Mafons*, to be actually in a State of Darknefs : However, I could never learn, that they ufe this Ceremony of Blindfolding in any of the numerous *Englifh Lodges*.

(*e*) Poffibly, there is but one *Lodge* of *Free-Mafons* at *Paris*, and fo that *venerable* Chief of this ancient *Order* officiates in Perfon. Here in *En-gland* each *Lodge* has its refpective Mafter and Wardens. The *Englifh* Right Worfhipfull *Grand-Mafter* is fcarce ever at the Trouble of *Makings*, except when the *Brother* be *Made*, is a Perfon of very eminent Degree, as *Brother* LORRAIN, now *Grand-Duke* of *Tufcany*, or fuch-like Grandees.

with his Officers, and the Body of Members, are affembled.

Hereupon the Grand-Mafter, from within, anfwers alfo with three Knocks (*f*), and orders the Door to be open'd.

The God-Father entering, fays; *He comes to prefent a Gentleman, whofe Name is* * * *, *and who defires to be receiv'd, as a Brother.*

Note, Both without and within the Chamber of Reception, there are divers Brothers, (*g*) with drawn Swords in

---

(*f*) By ftriking, with a neat little Mallet, pretty hard upon the Table. Every Mafter of a *Lodge* has one to ufe on all Occafions, as calling, *To Order, Silence, Charge, Drink,* or the like, all which he does by three great Knocks, as Paufes between the two latter Ones.

Note. Almoft every Thing in *Free-Mafonry* goes by the myfterious Number *Three.*

(*g*) In the *Englifh Lodges* generally they have only one *Brother,* who is a poor One, and guards the Door within-fide He has a fwinging Broad-Sword, in their Hands, ftanding Guard to keep off the Prophane. (*h*)

The Grand-Mafter, who wears round his Neck a blue Ribbon cut in Triangles, (*i*) fays, *Ask him, if he has a* Call? (*See the* Note *above.*)

Upon

Sword, naked in his Hand, and has, as I have been told, a Crown for his Evening's Trouble, befides Wine to drink, and a Pint Bottle home with him, if only a Lodge-Night; but at a *Making*, he partakes of the Feaft, and, together with the ufual Emoluments, has, in common with the other Brethren, and Vifiting-Brothers, a new White Leather-Apron, and two Pair of Gloves.

(*h*) Thus do *Free-Mafons* in *France*, it feems, ftile all fuch as are not of their Fraternity. And why fhould we wonder at that? Do not thofe of every Sect or Perfuafion, do the like, and even beftow far more opprobious Epithets?

(*i*) Here our Author quite puzzles me, fince I cannot devife what he can mean by this Ribbon cut into Triangles. Are thefe *French Free-Mafons*, Diffenters or Hereticks? With us, both Grand-Mafters and Grand-Wardens, nay all Mafters and Wardens, wear fine broad Ribbons, whereon are pendent upon their Breafts what they, particularly,

Upon this the God-Father, in Obedience to his Command, goes out to ask the said Question.

The Recipiendary having answer'd affirmatively, and his Reply being reported;

The Grand-Master then says, *Let the Candidate make his Entrance.*

He is hereupon introduc'd. Being come in, he is led about the Room, round a Space mark'd out upon the Floor with Chalk, within which is drawn a Sort of Representation, on two Columns, of the Ruins of *Solomon*'s Temple.

On the two Sides of this mark'd Space, are also figur'd out with Chalk

- a

larly stile their *Jewels*. These I have seen often enough. A Master's *Jewel* is the *Square*, a Senior Warden's, the *Level*, and a Junior Warden's the *Plumb-Rule*. So I know not what to make of this trianglified Ribbon.

a large J, and as large a B. The Explanation whereof is not given till after the Ceremony of Reception, or *Making* the *Brother*, is over.

And within the said Space stand three lighted Tapers, placed in a Triangle, whereon, at the Novice's Arrival, they sprinkle Gun-powder, or pounded Rosin, in order to frighten him by the Effort which their so doing produces. (*k*)

B   The

(*k*) The *French* being a People of peculiar Vivacity, as is well known, they have doubtless made great Improvements in *Masonry*, certainly with a laudable View of out-doing our Flegmatick Islanders, else why these Fire-Works, to shock and terrify the poor Novice? I could never learn, that either our *English*, or even the *Scotish* Masons, who, it seems, are Schismaticks in this, as well other Points, having ever had any Thing like this. Indeed, I have been assur'd, that the Reverend Mr. N———*n*, a Gentleman of a most happy Invention, once propos'd to a great Assembly of Brethren, the introducing such

Things

The Novice, or Recipiendary, having made three Turns round the *Lodge*, he is brought to the Weft End of that marked Space, as defcribed above, juft oppofite to the Grand-Mafter, who is ftanding behind a two-armed Chair whereon is a Book containing the Gofpel according to St. *John*.

Then

Things into *Makings* ; but that, on his Motion's being over-ruled, he took it into his Head to empoy his *Crackers* elfewhere, which is a Piece of Secret Hiftory perhaps known to few but myfelf. And here I muft take Leave to infert a merry Paffage, which I know to be Fact. The late Mr. *Pinkethman*, of facetious Memory, having been prevail'd on to become a Brother of the Society, was, in Order to his Initiation, conducted o a certain Tavern, where was held the *Lodge* whereof he was to enter himfelf a Member. Being left in the Kitchen over his Half Pint, ti'l his intended God-Father, with others, came to fetch him, a roguifh Drawer thruft the Salamander into the **Fire ;** which being in the Cook's Way, fhe angrily

Then fays the Grand-Mafter to the Novice, *Have you a Call?*

grily asks him, why he left it there? Why, an-fwer'd he, *Don't you know that we have a* Making *of* Free-Mafons *to Night?* Hah! cried poor *Pinky,* ftarting up, and ftaring as if bewitch'd, *What do you fay?* Making *and* Salamander? *Here you Sir, take my Reckoning.* At that Inftant the Bre-thren came down for him; but away ran *Pinky* and they after him; but no Perfuafions could bring him back, and fo the Fraternity irrecovera-bly loft a worthy Brother, who would infallibly have given them infinite Diverfion. As to the Reft, the only Method I could ever find yet taken by our *Englifh Mafons* to furprize, or terrify their new Brethren, or Novices, is this *viz.* immedi-ately on the Novice's firft Entrance (for they en-ter one by one, how many foever are *made* at once) the whole Body of the Brotherhood then prefent, more or lefs, being rang'd round the *Lodge,* chalked out, as above, in an oblong-Square, in due Order, that is, the *Mafter* in the *Eaft,* the two *Wardens* in the *Weft,* the *Fellow-Craft* in the *South,* and the *Enter'd-Prentices* in the *North,* all ready cloathed, *i. e.* with their white Gloves and Aprons on, they all at once with one Motion, clap their Right-hands hard on their Left-breafts, and

then

The Novice having replied, *Yes, Grand Master*; that Chief of *Free Masons* says; *Let him be shewed the Light; he has been depriv'd of it long enough.* (*l*)

Immediately thereupon his Eyes are unblinded, and he beholds the Brethren all ftanding in a Circle, with drawn Swords in their Hands. (*m*) Then he is made to advance at three Strides, or Paufes, quite up to a little low Stool at the Foot of the great Chair

then as hard or harder down on their Right-Skirts, againft their Aprons, which fudden Noife (added to the odd Accounts given relating to this myfterious Society, particularly by Women) fails not to ftartle the New-Comers · And undoubtedly it would operate more powerfully were they blindfolded, which Ceremony, as I hinted, is not here practifed.

(*l*) See the Note wherein Mention is made of the Darknefs they judge all Men to be in till they are *made*; i. e. become *Mafons*.

(*m*) This Article of Drawn-Swords I alfo take to be another Innovation, *a la Francoife.*

Chair behind which the Grand-Master is standing.

Then the Brother Orator *says* to the Novice, *You are going to be initiated into a most respectable Order, which is more serious, perhaps, than you imagine. It has not in it any Thing contrary to Law, to Religion, to our Sovereign, or to Morality. Our Venerable Grand Master will acquaint you with all I omit.*

After this, he is made to kneel with his right Knee bared upon the little Stool, holding up his left Foot off the Floor; while the Grand Master *says* to him.

You do promise never to write, ingrave or reveal the Secrets of Free Masons and Free-Masonry, but only to a Brother in a Lodge, and in Presence of the Venerable Grand Master.

They then strip open his Breast, to see

ſee whether he is not of the wrong
Sex, and apply to his left Pap the Point
of a Compaſs, open'd in a direct
Square, (which he himſelf muſt hold
there) and laying his right Hand on
the *Goſpel*, he pronounces theſe dicta-
ted Words; *viz.*

I promiſe this, under no leſs Penal-
ty, than having my Tongue pluck'd out,
my Heart torn from my Breaſt, my
Body burned and reduced to Aſhes, to be
caſt into the Wind, that I may never
more be ſpoken of among Men: So
help me God. (*n*)

They

(*n*) We have had this *Oath*, or *Solemn-Obli-*
gation of a *Maſon*, as they rather term it, printed more largely in ſome New's-Papers, and likewiſe in a Pamphlet; wherein the Author, a *Quon-*
dam-Maſon, has (as ſome of that Fraternity have
affirm'd) maliciouſly publiſh'd only juſt what
might make the Brotherhood ridiculous, and ſe-
creted ſuch Particulars as are truly grand, noble,
generous

They then oblige him to kifs the Book, and the Grand Mafter making him approach and ftand by him ; they clothe him, *i. e.* put on his *Free-Mafons* Apron (made of a white Skin) give him a Pair of Man's Gloves for himfelf, with another Pair for a Woman, to prefent the Perfon of that Sex for whom he has moft Efteem.

Next they explain to him the Meaning of thofe Letters J and B. which are within the Chalked Space, and which are the Symbol of their *Signs* whereby to know each other : *viz.* The J fignifies *Jakhin*, and the B fignifies *Boazes*, (i. e. *Jachin* and *Boaz.* See 1 *Kings* viii. 21.

Note, Thefe two Words are *Englifh;*

generous and beneficent : which (fay they) is a very *Un-mafonly* Procedure, and not at all acting upon the *Square.*

gliſh; (o) and they thus reprefent them in their *Signs* among themfelves; *viz*. They put their right Hand, open and extended, to the left Side of their Chin, and withdrawing it in a direct Line towards the Right, they ſtrike with it on the right Skirt of their Coat; which done they take each other by the ſame right Hand, mutually applying their Thumbs to their firſt Joint or Knuckle, of the Other's Fore-finger, pronouncing the Word *Jachin*, and then both ſtrike themſelves on the Breaſt with the ſame Hand.   After they again join their Hands, placing their Thumbs on the Knuckle

(o) Here this Diſcoverer is egregiouſly out; miſtaking *Hebrew* Words for *Engliſh* But indeed one need not wonder at finding ſuch Ignorance of Scripture among *Papiſts*, more eſpecially thoſe of the Laity.   Might he have peruſ'd the Bible, the firſt Book of *Kings* (as above) would have inſtructed him better

Knuckle of each other's Middle Finger, pronouncing the Word *Boaz*.

This Ceremony over, and its Meaning explain'd, *the* Recipiendary is ſtiled *Brother*, and they all ſit down at the Table, where, with the venerable Grand-Maſter's Permiſſion, the new Brother's Health is propoſed, each having before him a full Bottle.

When they are thus making ready to Booze, the Word is; *Let us have ſome Powder.* Thereupon they all riſe up. The Grand Maſter cries, *Charge;* and they all pour their Powder, *i. e.* Wine, into the Glaſſes. *Handle your Arms*, cries the Grand Maſter, and the new Brother's Health is toaſted, in doing which the Glaſſes are lifted to their Mouths at three Pauſes.

Then before ſetting down their empty Glaſſes on the Table, they put them to their left Breaſt, next to their

C   right

right Breaſt, and then with the Arm extended ſtrait forwards, with three Motions in all, which done, with three other Motions, or Pauſes, they ſet them perpendicularly down on the Table; and then clapping loudly with their Hands thrice, they thrice call out *Vivat*.

On the Table ſtand three large Wax Tapers in high Candleſticks, placed Triangular-wiſe. (*p*)

If accidentally they perceive, or fancy they perceive any ſuſpected Perſon introduced, or got in among them, it is ſignified to the others by ſaying,

(*p*) Theſe three Tapers (in grand and elegant gilded Candleſticks, made like Columns of ſome one of the five Orders of Architecture; they term their *Three Great Lights*; and if ask'd what theſe do repreſent, their Anſwer is, The Sun, the Moon, and the Master-Mason. They do, or ſhould ſtand due *Eaſt*, due *Weſt*, and due *South*.

faying, *It rains*; (*q*) thereby giving Notice, that every one muft be on his Guard, and talk no more like *Mafons*.

As it may poffibly happen, that fome of the *Profane* may have learned the *Signs* which denote *Jachin* and *Boaz*, in order to prevent all Surprize, in joyning Hands, as above, one fays to the other (in Cafe he fufpects him not to be really a *Brother*) J to which the other replies A. Then fays the firft C and is anfwer'd H. J fays the firft again; N cries the latter: Which Letters joined form the Word *Jachin*. (*r*)

C 2   The

(*q*) On fuch Occafions, they have alfo other Expreffions; as we often hear them fay, in mixed Companies, where any Thing relating to *Mafonry* is ftarted, *It drops, The Houfe is untiled*, &c.

(*r*) As this Article requires fome further Explication,

The fame Method is obferv'd with Refpect to the Word *Boaz*, by pronouncing alternately and fucceffively the Letters whereof it is compofed.

And

plication, I fhall endeavour to make it plainer and more familiar to the Reader. So (to ufe the Stile of our *French Mafons*) fince the *Brotherhood's* Signs, *&c.* are got out among fome of the *Profane*, they may be apt enough, when among real *Mafons*, to tip a *Sign* by way of Decoy.   Upon this, fome *Brother* anfwers with *another* (for it feems they have many of them) and perhaps beckons the *Stranger* afide, giving him his Hand, in order to receive alfo the *Token* or *Gripe*, as well as the *S.gn*.   If the *Stranger* is likewife right in that, then the *Brother*, to try him farther, fays, *If you are what you would be taken for, give me a* Word. The Stranger (many of whom have picked up even more than all that) ufually replies, artfully enough, *Give me* one, *and I will give you* another. Then fays the *Mafon*, *No, but I will* Letter *it with You*.   So as above.

But notwithftanding thefe and all other Difcoveries, that have been hitherto made of the *Myfteries* of *Mafonry*; yet it is ftill averr'd by 'em, that one Way excepted, there is no Poffibility that
                                                    their

And thefe are the chief *Signs* and *Tokens* whereby the True *Brethren* mutually know each other.

their whole and entire Magazine of *Secrets* fhou'd ever be divulged. Which is, for the *Fraternity* to have a general Meeting for that very Purpofe, and unanimoufly concur in penning down what is known among them; otherwife (fay they) the Thing is utterly impracticable, no one being ever yet found who was able, without being *prompted,* to anfwer even to a moderate Part of their *Catechifm*; which, by the Way fhould *prompt* them to be more perfect in their *Leffons* and not fuffer Themfelves to be outftript by *Children*; however, notwithftanding their boafted Affurances, their other darling *Secrets* may probably ftill be fhortly revealed, their *Myftical Emblems* explain'd to as mean Capacities as *Quarles*'s, and all their *hidden Works* of *Darknefs* in due Time *fee the Light.*

The

The Free Masons Reception in Foreign Parts.

From *Paris, March* 10. 1737.

THE sudden Encrease of the Society of *Free Masons* in *France* has given such Offence, that the King forbid their Meeting at any of their Lodges ; nor would the States of *Holland* suffer them.

From *Rome, July* 18. 1730.

The Society of *Free Masons,* lately detected at *Florence,* makes a great Noise : They pass there for *Quietists* ; but here it is said they are of the *Epicurean* Sect, and that there are no Laws too severe to deal with them. The Pope sent the Father-Inquisitor of that Office, Post to *Florence,* in Order to prosecute them, at the Request of the Great Duke of *Tuscany,* who was absolutely resolv'd to extirpate the whole Sect.

As his Highness is since dead, and the Duke of Lorrain, *who was made a Free Mason, in* England, *is to succeed, this Prosecution may not go far.*

The Free Masons *Apology.*

As it was Published at Paris, *in* March, 1737.

THAT the *Views* the *Free Ma-sons* propose to themselves are the most pure and inoffensive, and tend only to promote such Qualities in them as may form good Citizens, and zealous Subjects; faithful to their Prince, to their Country, and to their Friends: That the Name of *Free Mason* is far from being an insignificant Title: That the Duty it prescribes to those that bear it, is to endeavour to erect Temples for Virtue, and Dungeons for Vice: That he is by no Means afraid of violating the Secret imposed

upon

upon them in publifhing, That their principal Defign is to reftore to the Earth the Reign of *Aftræa*, and revive the Time of *Rhea*.   He affures the *Fair*, that the whole Brotherhood is full of Refpect and Veneration for them; but that thefe Sentiments are not exempt from Fear; and that Fear obliges the *Free Mafons* to exclude the Sex from their Affemblies: which he concludes, ought not to provoke the Indignation of thofe who are the Objects of it: To prevent fuch an Effect, they need only recollect from whom *Adam* receiv'd the Apple: Sad Prefent! Since had it not been for that fatal Apple, *Adam* would have remained the firft Free Mafon.

The

FREE MASONS *a dangerous Society.*

From the CRAFTSMAN, April 16. 1737.

Mr. *D'anvers,*

AMongst all the various Instances of our Advantages over other Nations in Point of *Liberty,* there is one so very remarkable, that it deserves your most serious Consideration ; I mean the Toleration of that mysterious Society call'd *Free Masons,* who have been lately suppress'd not only in *France,* but in *Holland,* as a dangerous Race of Men ; (*See p.* 22.) whereas here they are permitted to hold their private Meetings in every Part of the Town, and even to appear in Publick Procession with the Ensigns of their Order.

Indeed, I have often wonder'd that they have not been laid under some Restraints even in *England;* for tho' *our present most excellent Ministers* have always preserved a sacred Regard to *Liberty,* I think no Government ought to suffer such clandestine Assemblies, where Plots against the State may be carried on, under the Pretence of a *Brotherly* Love and *good Fellowship.*

D   The

The *Act of Toleration* does not allow of private *Conventicles*, even in Cases of *Conscience*, but injoins that all *Places of divine Worship*, shall be not only *licensed*, but *publick*. Shall more Indulgence be granted to his *incomprehensible Fraternity*, who do not pretend, as far as I ever heard, to plead *Conscience*, or any *publick Emolument* in their Behalf?

They derive their Original, as I am inform'd, from the Building of *Babel*, which every Body knows was an audacious Attempt against *Heaven*; insomuch that God himself thought fit to defeat their Design by the *Confusion of Tongues*, that such impious Offenders might not understand one another. But, on the contrary, our *modern Masons* pretend to an *universal, dumb Language*, by which People of all Nations upon the Face of the Earth, who are initiated into their Mysteries, can easily converse together, by the Help of *certain Signs*, known only to themselves.

It is likewise said that by the *same Signs* they can oblige any of their Brethren to leave off their Work, and follow them wherever they please; a Power which may be some Time or other turned to a very ill Use.

The *Concord* and *Unanimity*, which reigns so remarkably amongſt them, is very ſurprizing; for though they are compoſed of all *Nations*, *Parties* and *Religions*, We are told that there hath not happened the leaſt Quarrel or Diſturbance in any of their Aſſemblies.

That *impenetrable Secrecy*, for which they are ſo famous, is likewiſe Matter of juſt Suſpicion, and ſeems to indicate that there is ſomething in their *nocturnal Rites* and *Ceremonies*, which they are afraid of having diſcovered.

For this Reaſon, they not only lock themſelves into the Room, where they meet, and ſuffer none to wait upon them, except *Brethren*; but upon all extraordinary Occaſions, a *Centinel* is placed at the Outſide of the Door, with a *drawn Sword* in his Hand, to prevent all Diſcoveries.

This is not the only Mark of their being a *military Order*; for it is very obſervable that they give their *chief Officer* the Title of GRAND-MASTER; in Imitation, I preſume, of the *Knights of Malta*; nay, he hath a *Sword of State* carried before him, almoſt as large, and richly ornamented as That of his Majeſty. This Sword was preſented fented to them, as I am inform'd by a *great R man Catholick Peer*.——With what View I fhall not take upon me pofitively to determine.

There feems likewife to be fomething emblematical in the *Gloves* and *Aprons* ; a *Gove* is only another Word for a *Gauntlet*, which is a *Piece of Armour for the Hands*. An *Apro*, indeed, is a proper Badge of *Mafonry*, in the literal Senfe, but it is likewife a Term in *Gunnery* for a flat Piece of Lead to cover the *Touch-hole of a Cannon*, when it is loaded; and I leave my *Superiors* to judge whether it may not be made Ufe of by our *Free Mafons* to typify fomething like it.

It farther deferves Notice how artfully they have difperfed themfelves, in *different Lodges* through all Parts of the Kingdom; and particularly in *this great Metropolis*; as if it were on Purpofe to beat up for *Volunteers*, in which they not only admit *Turks*, *Jews*, *Infidels*, but even *Jacobites*, *Nonjurors*, and *Papifts* themfelves.

They keep their Proceedings fo very private, that it is impoffible to guefs what *Seal of Secrecy* they have invented, which is able to tie up the Mouths of fuch Multitudes,

tudes, whom the moſt ſolemn Oaths could not bind, upon any other Occaſion.

I ſiſh it may not be ſomewhat like *that horrid Obligation,* which *Catiline* adminiſter'd to his *Fellow-Conſpirators.*

Upon the Whole, *this myſterious Society* hath too much the Air of an *Inquiſition,* where every Thing is tranſacted in the Dark.

It may be ſaid, that a *learned and worthy Divine of the Church of England,* hath long ago publiſh'd the *Inſtitution of the Free Maſons,* which contain nothing but what is perfectly innocent, and prove them to be rather a *whimſical* than a *dangerous* and *formidable Sect.* But I muſt obſerve that *this Book* ſeems deſign'd rather to *amuſe* than *inform* the World; for it is not to be ſuppoſed that he would reveal *thoſe boaſted Myſteries,* in which the very Eſſence of their *Society* conſiſts.

But the moſt material Argument is, that there are ſo many of the *Nobility, Gentry,* and even the *Clergy,* of the moſt undoubted Affection to his Majeſty's Perſon, Family, and Government, in *this Society;* that as it will be impoſſible to carry on any wicked Deſigns againſt him without their Knowledge,

ledge, so it cannot be supposed that they will concur in them, or conceal them. But, with all due Deference to *these Hon.* and *Rev. Persons,* I beg Leave to give my Opinion, that *this Argument* is very fallacious, and upon which we can have no sure Dependance; for I apprehend the *Obligation,* which the *Free Masons* take to be of such a Nature, that the *blackest Conspiracies,* or *Machinations,* will not allow them to break through it. Besides, how can we be sure that *those Persons,* who are known to be *well affected,* are let into all their *Mysteries?* They make no Scruple to acknowledge that there is a Distinction between *Prentices* and *Master-Masons;* and who knows whether they may not have an higher Order of *Cabalists,* who keep the *grand Secret* of all entirely to themselves?

It may be ask'd, perhaps, in what *Plots,* or *ill Designs* of any Sort, they have been engag'd since the first Foundation of *their Society?* This Question is not easily answered; for their Principles and Actions are so unfathomable, that nobody can say with Certainty, in what they are concern'd, or not concern'd; but I cannot help thinking them at the Bottom of *one Affair,* I mean
the

the late Tumult at *Edinburgh*, and the Murder of Captain *Porteous*; which was concerted and executed with fo much *Unanimity* and *Secrecy*, that none but a Mob of *Free Mafons* could be guilty of it, without the Difcovery of *one Perfon* in fo numerous a Multitude as were concern'd in the Perpetration of that *atrocious Fact*.

I am glad to hear that a *Law* is likely to pafs in the Nature of the *Black-Act*, for preventing *fuch Riots*, for the future, by trying the Authors of them in *England*; for if the *Scots* will not find one another guilty, there is all the Reafon in the World they fhould be try'd by an *impartial Jury*, who know nothing of *Them*, or *their Characters*; and I hope to fee the *Free Mafons* included in the *fame Bill*; for they may be properly faid *to go in Difguife*.

I know *thefe Men* are generally look'd upon, in *England*, as a Parcel of idle People, who meet together only to make merry, and play fome ridiculous Pranks; but it is very plain that the wife Government of *France* and *Holland* look upon them in a very different Light; and I humbly hope to fee my own Country follow the *Example* of the latter, at leaft, by fuppreffing fuch *dangerous Affemblies.*   But

But if a *total Suppreßion* ſhould be thought inconſiſtent with our *free Conſtitution* and moſt incomparable *Government*, I have an Alternative to offer ; which is to lay a double Tax upon all *Free Maſons*, as there hath been ſo many Years upon the *Papiſts*.

I flatter myſelf that this Scheme will not prove diſagreeable, at preſent, when *great Sums of Money* are wanted, and *Ways and Means* are ſo very hard to be found. I am ſure, it will be more acceptable to the Generality of Mankind, or at leaſt of Womankind, than the *Reduction of Intereſt of Three per Cent.* without any *Redemption of Taxes*; for as the *Ladies* have a very bad Opinion of the *Free Maſons*, and are incapable of being admitted into *that Order*, they will never complain of any Tax being laid upon *keep,a* a Secret, which they are not let into themſelves.

I am, Sir, &c.

JACHIN

F I N I S.

CPSIA information can be obtained at www.ICGtesting.com
Printed in the USA
LVOW082318300312

275510LV00011B/116/P

9 781170 268032